These dreams
belong to:

RP Studio™
Hachette Book Group
1290 Avenue of the Americas, New York, NY 10104
www.runningpress.com
@Running_Press

First Edition: April 2024

Published by RP Studio, an imprint of Hachette Book Group, Inc. The RP Studio name
and logo are trademarks of Hachette Book Group, Inc.

Running Press books may be purchased in bulk for business, educational, or promotional
use. For more information, please contact your local bookseller or the Hachette Book
Group Special Markets Department at Special.Markets@hbgusa.com.

The publisher is not responsible for websites (or their content) that are not owned by
the publisher.

Design by Jenna McBride.

ISBN: 978-0-7624-8129-3

Printed in China

1010

10 9 8 7 6 5 4 3 2 1

THE
DREAMGATE
GUIDED JOURNAL

NURTURE YOUR DREAMS
AND WAKING LIFE

CREATED FOR YOU BY
DANIELLE NOEL

RP STUDIO
PHILADELPHIA

Rest with the center of your heart.

Deepen into the present moment.

Surrender to the flow that emerges through your fingertips.

Write like no one is watching.

Stay in alignment with your truth.

Your words have power.

Your heart is a compass.

The pages are here for you.

CONTENTS

INTRODUCTION

✧ ✧ ✧

Welcome, dear seeker. This book is here to enhance your own sweet exploration of dreamwork, shared through a series of guided pages. As with *The Dreamgate Oracle*, this journal is designed to be used at the cusp of your waking hours—before you head to sleep and shortly after you rise. Its purpose is to not only provide you with a supportive container to pour out your heart and reflect on life, but to also help unlock your own powerful revelations. No matter how great or small, let each transmission you write and express open a greater dialogue with your inner self. Let your ongoing discoveries strengthen your intuition (and imagination) even more, as you weave the threads of your dream-stories together. As you journey within, I hope you unlock even more Dreamgates of your own, as you tap into the flow of your wisdom and wonder.

YOUR INNER JOURNEY

One of the greatest lessons I have taken away from dreamwork is that each **dream** and perceived **symbol** can be totally unique in its translation—**just as the person who houses the experience is a completely unique individual on this planet.** Like fingerprints, no two dream interpretations will ever be alike, so they will always be defined through the eyes of the traveler. We may see universal similarities within dream analysis teachings and may also seek outside sources to aid our interpretations. These can be incredibly helpful in finding our bearings when it comes to reading our dreams, but there is often more at play within our own personal experiences and stories. When it comes to dream analysis, what works for one person may not apply to another, so we each need to find our own way of deciphering the clues we are presented with. And we must trust our inner compass to guide us as we navigate forward.

This journal is unique in its format, as it is also designed to incorporate the cards of your oracle, to help you establish a deeper dream analysis. As you shuffle and explore, you may choose to blend in your own oracle spreads or one-card touchstones for your daily questions. Take note of the themes and visuals that surface as you tap into this process. Each oracle key offers a portal that is imbued with gentle wisdom to activate your own discoveries.

The prompts that are shared throughout *The Dreamgate Oracle*, and this book, are also expressed to help you illuminate any shadows in your life that may require a dose of healing or support. Many of these queries go deep, encouraging you to also tap into your own divine guidance. There are also added prompts for self-care support, and gentle reminders that it's okay to take some extra time for yourself when needed.

Feel free to use *The Dreamgate Oracle* for your explorations, and to consider bringing in other decks, oracles, and tools as well. The questions and prompts contained in this journal can inspire your self-understanding with the guidance of any card that speaks to your soul.

SIGNIFICATOR CARD

Similar to a one-card reading, you may want to pull a single card to open up a dialogue with your dzream reflections. This helps anchor in the potency of what may be rising or transmuting within your particular reading for that day. Before you head to sleep, it can also be helpful to pull a single card to enhance your transition into dreamland. This card can be used as a focal point for meditation and relaxation, or to help conclude the energy of your day. Perhaps there is also a lingering theme or message being shared through this key. Let your heart guide you as you become comfortable with this simple practice.

ORACLE PROMPTS

AKASHIC FLOW

TAPPING IN · ANCIENT LIBRARY

NEW DISCOVERIES · AWAKENING

I release the paradigms that block my truth.

I am open to new ways of learning and receiving.

✦ DREAM REFLECTIONS ✦

How am I being guided to grow, learn, or evolve?

_____

_____

_____

_____

_____

_____

_____

_____

_____

_____

What new wisdom teachings am I yearning for at this time?

_____

_____

_____

_____

_____

_____

_____

_____

_____

_____

ANCHORING IN

PRANA · ENERGY MEDICINE

BODY TEMPLE · VIBRATIONAL HEALING · KA

I am a holy vessel.

I am a receiver, transmitter, and transmuter.

✧ DREAM REFLECTIONS ✧

How can I tune in to my energy body more?

_____

_____

_____

_____

_____

_____

_____

_____

_____

What am I dreaming of expressing, healing, or releasing at this time?

_____

_____

_____

_____

_____

_____

_____

_____

_____

_____

ANCIENT MUSE

SOUL TRUTHS · DEEP INSPIRATION

FAMILIAR RESONANCE · HIGHER SELF

I am the Ancient Muse.

I am a Visionary.

✧ DREAM REFLECTIONS ✧

What new ideas, visions, or dreams now bloom within me?

_____

_____

_____

_____

_____

_____

_____

_____

_____

_____

How am I being called to deepen into my own unique nature?

_____

_____

_____

_____

_____

_____

_____

_____

_____

_____

ANIMAL KIN

SWEET FAMILIARS · MESSENGERS

COMPANIONS · FREE REIN

I am open to receive.

I trust my instincts.

✧ DREAM REFLECTIONS ✧

How can I tap into my wildest expressions?

_____

_____

_____

_____

_____

_____

_____

_____

_____

_____

How can I learn from the animal kin?

_____

_____

_____

_____

_____

_____

_____

_____

_____

_____

BELIEVING IS SEEING

IMAGINATION · BEYOND THE VEIL

INNER CHILD · PLAY

I am ready to activate my inner magic.

I am open to the power of my imagination.

✧ DREAM REFLECTIONS ✧

Where in my life can I visualize more magic, wonder, awe, and excitement? How can I encourage this exploration as a more active practice in my life?

_____
_____
_____
_____
_____
_____
_____
_____
_____

Where am I holding resistance to what I cannot see, but wish to believe?

_____
_____
_____
_____
_____
_____
_____
_____
_____
_____

BETWEEN WORLDS

TWILIGHT DREAM · PSYCHIC WISDOM · CUSP OF REALITY

REVELATIONS · PARALLEL WORLDS · ETHERIC BRIDGE

I am open to receive new wisdom teachings.

I know there is more to be revealed.

✧ DREAM REFLECTIONS ✧

What new dreams or visions call out to me from beyond?

_____
_____
_____
_____
_____
_____
_____
_____
_____
_____

What unseen truths do I sense today?

_____
_____
_____
_____
_____
_____
_____
_____
_____
_____
_____

CELESTIAL TEMPLE

DREAM INCUBATION · INTENTIONS · YOU ARE NOT ALONE

THE UNIVERSE · COSMIC DOWNLOADS · DIVINE TRUTHS

I am ready to tap into higher planes of wisdom.

I let the universe show me the way.

What is my soul yearning to learn?

_____
_____
_____
_____
_____
_____
_____
_____
_____
_____

How and where can I tune in to the language of the Divine?

_____
_____
_____
_____
_____
_____
_____
_____
_____
_____
_____

CHOOSE YOUR ADVENTURE

LUCID DREAMS · CONSCIOUS DISCOVERIES

MANIFESTATION · ONEIRONAUTICS

I am always able to learn the language of my dreams.

I am ready to enhance my waking life.

✧ DREAM REFLECTIONS ✧

What is my dreamy intention for tonight or today?

_____
_____
_____
_____
_____
_____
_____
_____
_____
_____

How am I being guided to awaken my living dreams or desires?

_____
_____
_____
_____
_____
_____
_____
_____
_____
_____
_____

DAYDREAM BELIEVER

SEEDS OF DISCOVERY · FREE-FLOWING THOUGHTS

SOUL MESSAGES · DREAMY SOLUTIONS

I am open to my inner visions.

I am lost and found in my imagination.

✧ DREAM REFLECTIONS ✧

When my mind rests, what visions automatically arise?

_____
_____
_____
_____
_____
_____
_____
_____
_____
_____

Am I holding on to anything at this time?

_____
_____
_____
_____
_____
_____
_____
_____
_____
_____

DEEP REST

SHIFTING GEARS · DISCONNECT AND UNPLUG

RECHARGE AND REPAIR · EMPATHIC RETREAT

I am always able to reset my steps.

I am discovering new ways to relax.

✧ DREAM REFLECTIONS ✧

What kind of deep rest am I now being encouraged to tap into more?

_____

_____

_____

_____

_____

_____

_____

_____

_____

_____

What do I find most relaxing, nourishing, and calming in life?

_____

_____

_____

_____

_____

_____

_____

_____

_____

_____

THE DESERT

CROSSING THE THRESHOLD · AUTHENTIC SELF

TRANSCENDENCE · GENESIS · COURAGE

I am ready to find myself.

I let go of what I resist.

✧ DREAM REFLECTIONS ✧

What do I prioritize in life, above all else?

_____

_____

_____

_____

_____

_____

_____

_____

_____

_____

How have I learned to rise above the obstacles I experience?

_____

_____

_____

_____

_____

_____

_____

_____

_____

_____

_____

DIVE IN

GREEN LIGHT AHEAD · SPONTANEITY

ADVENTURE · INTUITIVE JUMPS · NEW BEGINNINGS

I am ready to take this leap of faith.

I am making room for new experiences.

✧ DREAM REFLECTIONS ✧

Where are the green lights guiding me now?

_____
_____
_____
_____
_____
_____
_____
_____
_____
_____

If I had no fear, what would I do?

_____
_____
_____
_____
_____
_____
_____
_____
_____
_____
_____

DOORS OF PERCEPTION

CHOICES · ILLUSIONS · OPPORTUNITIES

WISHES · INNER PATHWAYS · INDEPENDENCE

I am ready to make my own decision.

I make soul choices out of fulfillment.

How can I let go of my internalized pressures or expectations?

_____

_____

_____

_____

_____

_____

_____

_____

_____

_____

What choices can I make to enhance my life?

_____

_____

_____

_____

_____

_____

_____

_____

_____

_____

_____

DREAMY ESCAPE

WANDERLUST · HIDDEN TREASURES

LOOKING GLASS · CONSCIOUS DREAMING · SOJOURN

I embrace this simple exercise to calm my mind.

I am able to visualize and inspire my dreams.

✧ DREAM REFLECTIONS ✧

How would I richly describe my own dreamy escape today?

_____
_____
_____
_____
_____
_____
_____
_____
_____
_____

How would I visually describe my current state of being as a Dreamgate?

_____
_____
_____
_____
_____
_____
_____
_____
_____
_____

DUALITY

PARADIGM SHIFT · CHOICES · EARTH LESSONS

EQUILIBRIUM · BALANCE · TEMPERANCE

I can see the beauty of the in-between.

I am open to receive a whole new understanding.

Where can I seek out more equilibrium and balance?

_____

_____

_____

_____

_____

_____

_____

_____

_____

_____

How can I learn to soften or strengthen more?

_____

_____

_____

_____

_____

_____

_____

_____

_____

_____

EARTH-WALK

REORIENTATION · ANCHORING IN

COLLECTIVE WISDOM · BIG PICTURE · NATURAL HEALING

I see the interconnectedness of all life.

I am walking myself home each day. I am of the earth.

✧ DREAM REFLECTIONS ✧

How can I connect more with my own earth-walk?

_____

_____

_____

_____

_____

_____

_____

_____

_____

_____

What is my earthly spirit yearning for at this time?

_____

_____

_____

_____

_____

_____

_____

_____

_____

_____

_____

ELEMENTALS

DREAMLAND LORE · OTHERWORLD

EARTH SPIRITS · UNSEEN POWERS

I am ready to discover hidden truths.

I am open to the subtle, elemental realms.

✧ DREAM REFLECTIONS ✧

How can I connect more with my own natural Fae wisdom?

_____

_____

_____

_____

_____

_____

_____

_____

_____

_____

What am I yearning to discover in the otherworld?

_____

_____

_____

_____

_____

_____

_____

_____

_____

_____

_____

ENCHANTED FOREST

ACTIVATION CODES · GREEN HEALING · DEEP BREATH

NERVOUS SYSTEM SUPPORT · FOREST BATHING · GROUNDING

I am ready to let my pressures melt away.

I am always able to return to my breath.

✧ DREAM REFLECTIONS ✧

How can I connect more with my breath and heart?

_____
_____
_____
_____
_____
_____
_____
_____
_____
_____

What does my own inner forest look like?

_____
_____
_____
_____
_____
_____
_____
_____
_____
_____
_____

FAMILIAR STEPS

RECURRING DREAMS · CONTINUUM

RECLAIMED TRUTHS · HEALING · FULFILLMENT

I am open to the callings of my soul.

I am always attracting my highest potential.

✧ DREAM REFLECTIONS ✧

Is there any unfinished or unresolved business in my life?

_____

_____

_____

_____

_____

_____

_____

_____

_____

What familiar dreams, visions, or desires am I missing?

_____

_____

_____

_____

_____

_____

_____

_____

_____

_____

GENTLE DRIFT

THERE IS NO NEED TO RUSH · GO WITH THE FLOW

TRUST THE JOURNEY · SLOWING DOWN

I trust in the timing of this situation.

I can always move at a gentle pace.

How and where am I being encouraged to slow down?

_____
_____
_____
_____
_____
_____
_____
_____
_____
_____

Where in my life do things feel a bit too fast?

_____
_____
_____
_____
_____
_____
_____
_____
_____
_____

THE GOLDEN HOUR

THE GREAT CENTRAL SUN · TRANSMUTING BLOCKAGES

POSITIVE OMENS · CIRCADIAN RHYTHM SUPPORT

I am ready to replenish the sunlight of my heart.

I am making time for my own renewal.

✦ DREAM REFLECTIONS ✦

Where in my life am I needing an added dose of replenishment or renewal?

_____

_____

_____

_____

_____

_____

_____

_____

_____

_____

What can I celebrate at this time?

_____

_____

_____

_____

_____

_____

_____

_____

_____

_____

HARMONICS

VIBRATIONAL MEDICINE · SHARED RESONANCE

SOUND HEALING · MUSIC · NATURAL TONES

I align with the sounds that sing to my soul.

I speak and express with a high vibration.

✧ DREAM REFLECTIONS ✧

Are there any natural sounds I would like to explore?

_____

_____

_____

_____

_____

_____

_____

_____

_____

_____

How is the quality of my own self-talk and expressions?

_____

_____

_____

_____

_____

_____

_____

_____

_____

_____

_____

HEART ACTIVATION

SELF-LOVE • FOLLOWING YOUR BLISS

YOU MATTER • RESTORATION

I am ready to love myself, inside and out.

I am beautiful, beloved, and truly amazing.

What can I do today to celebrate my beautiful, wonderful self?

_____

_____

_____

_____

_____

_____

_____

_____

_____

_____

How am I being guided toward more self-love?

_____

_____

_____

_____

_____

_____

_____

_____

_____

_____

HIDDEN PORTAL

ALTERNATE ROUTES · LOOK CLOSER

RESILIENCE · A PATH LESS TRAVELED · CREATIVE SOLUTIONS

I am ready to step outside of expectations.

I can always adjust my view of each situation.

✦ DREAM REFLECTIONS ✦

Where am I being guided? What new experiences am I being drawn to?

_____
_____
_____
_____
_____
_____
_____
_____
_____
_____

What direction have I been resisting but wanting to move toward?

_____
_____
_____
_____
_____
_____
_____
_____
_____
_____
_____

HOLD THE LIGHT

LEMURIA · ANCIENT MEMORIES

SENSITIVE GIFTS · DREAMING A NEW WORLD · I REMEMBER

I am ready to surrender to new wisdom.

I am returning.

✧ DREAM REFLECTIONS ✧

How can I celebrate my sensitive nature more?

_____

_____

_____

_____

_____

_____

_____

_____

_____

_____

How can I see the world around me from a higher perspective?

_____

_____

_____

_____

_____

_____

_____

_____

_____

HOLY RENEWAL

DEATH · REBIRTH · CREATION

CYCLES OF HEALING · INITIATION · METAMORPHOSES

I am capable of healing.

I am always moving forward.

✧ DREAM REFLECTIONS ✧

What new initiations am I moving through?

_____

_____

_____

_____

_____

_____

_____

_____

_____

What have the deepest challenges I've faced taught me? How have I grown from these experiences?

_____

_____

_____

_____

_____

_____

_____

_____

_____

INNER EYE

PINEAL ACTIVATION · ILLUMINATION

PSYCHIC BRIDGE · THIRD EYE

Where I place my attention is where my power flows.

I am open to the wisdom of my own intuition.

✧ DREAM REFLECTIONS ✧

What can I do to support my inner wisdom more?

_____

_____

_____

_____

_____

_____

_____

_____

How is my inner eye guiding me at this time? How can I trust myself more?

_____

_____

_____

_____

_____

_____

_____

_____

INNER MAGIC

YOUR VIBRATION IS RISING • INCREASED ENERGY

POWER • SOWING SEEDS • YOU ARE BRILLIANT

I am ready to encompass the magic I hold within.

I let go of anything that blocks my power.

✧ DREAM REFLECTIONS ✧

How can I exude more confidence and inner strength?

_____

_____

_____

_____

_____

_____

_____

_____

_____

Where do my own strengths and gifts lie? How am I being encouraged to show myself more?

_____

_____

_____

_____

_____

_____

_____

_____

_____

KINDRED SPIRITS

VIBRATIONAL MAGNETISM · SOUL FAMILY

EARTH LESSONS · UNCONDITIONAL LOVE

I am treasuring the gift of friendship.

I am open to growing with each relationship.

✧ DREAM REFLECTIONS ✧

What have the relationships in my life taught me?

_____

_____

_____

_____

_____

_____

_____

_____

_____

Are there any connections in my life that may require some healing?

_____

_____

_____

_____

_____

_____

_____

_____

_____

MESSENGERS

DIVINE ORCHESTRATION · GUARDIANS

SIGNS · CALLING IN SUPPORT · SHINING ONES

I am Divinely protected and seen.

I am open to the guidance of my angelic allies.

✧ DREAM REFLECTIONS ✧

How can I take note of the miracles in my life more?

_____

_____

_____

_____

_____

_____

_____

_____

_____

What am I yearning to ask for at this time?

_____

_____

_____

_____

_____

_____

_____

_____

_____

_____

MOON CASTING

NATURAL RHYTHMS · CULTIVATION · MANIFESTATION

SERENITY · MAGIC · DREAMWORK

I am always regulating more harmony.

I am connecting with my natural rhythms.

✧ DREAM REFLECTIONS ✧

What am I hoping to release, heal, create, or enhance at the next new moon?

_____

_____

_____

_____

_____

_____

_____

_____

_____

What am I wanting to reinforce or strengthen at the next full moon?

_____

_____

_____

_____

_____

_____

_____

_____

_____

THE MOUNTAIN

OBSTACLES AHEAD · OVERCOMING FEAR

PERSEVERANCE · KEEP GOING

I am ready to rise above this challenge.

I am growing with each and every step.

✧ DREAM REFLECTIONS ✧

How can I adjust my view of and approach to the challenges I am faced with?

_____

_____

_____

_____

_____

_____

_____

_____

_____

_____

Where are the mountains appearing in my life at this time?

_____

_____

_____

_____

_____

_____

_____

_____

_____

_____

MOVE WITH GRACE

OPTIMIZED LIGHT · INNER AND OUTER FORGIVENESS

CELEBRATE YOURSELF · FULL HEART, FULL SPIRIT

I move with integrity.

I act, speak, and express with kindness.

✧ DREAM REFLECTIONS ✧

How can I move with more grace in my life?

_____

_____

_____

_____

_____

_____

_____

_____

_____

How can I identify the grace around and within me more?

_____

_____

_____

_____

_____

_____

_____

_____

_____

MULTIVERSE

EXPAND YOUR MIND · REFINE YOUR FOCUS · PORTAL

QUANTUM TRAVEL · THE BIG PICTURE · MACROCOSM

I am ready to discover my own cosmological truths.

I see the greater picture.

✧ DREAM REFLECTIONS ✧

How can I expand my scope of this world and learn more from the mysteries of the cosmos?

_____
_____
_____
_____
_____
_____
_____
_____
_____

What is clouding my view of the life I desire?

_____
_____
_____
_____
_____
_____
_____
_____
_____
_____
_____

MYSTIC KEY

PATTERNS IN THE SUBTLE REALMS • TIME-KEYS

SOUL SYMBOLS • SYNCHRONICITY • SINGULARITIES

I weave the subtle threads of my story.

I trust the divine clues.

✧ DREAM REFLECTIONS ✧

How can I be more open to the signs around me?

_____

_____

_____

_____

_____

_____

_____

_____

_____

_____

Where have the signs or synchronicities shown up for me so far?

_____

_____

_____

_____

_____

_____

_____

_____

_____

_____

NOSTALGIC RELEASE

HEALING THE PAST • RELATIONSHIPS • SENSORY MEMORIES

ECHOES OF TIME • KARMIC LESSONS

I am ready to let go of the shadows of my past.

I am always healing, in every moment.

✧ DREAM REFLECTIONS ✧

Are there any memories or connections from my past that require some healing or forgiveness?

_____

_____

_____

_____

_____

_____

_____

_____

_____

Is there anything that I am still holding on to from my past that may be blocking my progress with something?

_____

_____

_____

_____

_____

_____

_____

_____

_____

PYRAMID

AMPLIFICATION · HARMONIC RESONANCE

COSMIC UNION

I am ready to call in more balance.

I am building strong foundations.

✧ DREAM REFLECTIONS ✧

How can I nourish my mind, body, and spirit more?

_____

_____

_____

_____

_____

_____

_____

_____

Where do I require more structure, balance, or strength at this time?

_____

_____

_____

_____

_____

_____

_____

_____

_____

_____

QUEST

GOALS • DEEP SHIFTS • CARVING OUT CHANGE

SENSORY TRUTHS • INNER JOURNEY • DESIRE

I am ready to follow my bliss.

I always listen to the subtle feelings within.

✧ DREAM REFLECTIONS ✧

What excites me? What brings me joy? What makes me laugh? What makes me truly happy?

You may also change all of the above with *who* or *where*—in your own words.

REFLECTIONS OF TIME

SURRENDER · CYCLES OF CHANGE · UNEARTHING

UPHEAVAL · LESSONS

I move toward my light.

I surrender to the great mysteries of life.

✦ DREAM REFLECTIONS ✦

Where and how am I being encouraged to surrender more?

_____

_____

_____

_____

_____

_____

_____

_____

_____

_____

How have my choices been reflected back to me?

_____

_____

_____

_____

_____

_____

_____

_____

_____

_____

SACRED CAVE

SPIRITUAL GROWTH · PERIOD OF GESTATION

INTROSPECTION

I am ready to face my deepest self.

I am open to the visions that wish to emerge.

✧ DREAM REFLECTIONS ✧

Where in my life am I being guided to retreat and grow?

_____
_____
_____
_____
_____
_____
_____
_____
_____
_____

Where is my own metaphoric cave in my life right now?

_____
_____
_____
_____
_____
_____
_____
_____
_____
_____
_____

SANCTUARY

CURATE YOUR REALM · SACRED SPACE

ALTAR · HAVEN

I love reflecting my heart into the spaces I inhabit.

I find magic and fulfillment in my creative surroundings.

How can I enhance my own sacred spaces?

_____

_____

_____

_____

_____

_____

_____

_____

_____

What can I celebrate, refresh, or build at this time?

_____

_____

_____

_____

_____

_____

_____

_____

_____

SECRET GARDEN

PLANTING NEW SEEDS · HIDDEN DREAMS

NOURISHMENT · STEPS

I am ready to plant new creative seeds.

I deserve to bloom in every way.

✧ DREAM REFLECTIONS ✧

What new growth am I suppressing or needing to release?

_____

_____

_____

_____

_____

_____

_____

_____

_____

_____

What can I begin seeding, planting, and nourishing within my life?

_____

_____

_____

_____

_____

_____

_____

_____

_____

_____

SHADOW KEY

SHADOW WORK · INNER WATERS

DISCLOSURE · EMOTIONAL HEALING

I am ready to soothe my shadows.

I am open to what is coming to light.

✧ DREAM REFLECTIONS ✧

How can I be softer with myself as I look within?

_____

_____

_____

_____

_____

_____

_____

_____

_____

Are there any inner or outer shadows in my life that seek some healing or love?

_____

_____

_____

_____

_____

_____

_____

_____

_____

SOOTHING WATERS

INTENTION • CLEARING BLOCKAGES

ENERGETIC HYGIENE • ESSENCE

I am ready to replenish and recharge my life.

I clear away all that blocks my happiness.

✧ DREAM REFLECTIONS ✧

What am I being called to cleanse, purge, or release?

_____
_____
_____
_____
_____
_____
_____
_____
_____
_____

What intention would I like to imbue in my own waters, inner and outer?

_____
_____
_____
_____
_____
_____
_____
_____
_____
_____
_____

SPIRAL OF INCARNATION

PAST LIVES · SPIRAL OF LIFE

LESSONS · SOUL BLUEPRINT · KARMIC PATTERNS

I am ready to hear the call of my soul.

I see the patterns as lessons.

✧ DREAM REFLECTIONS ✧

What experiences or memories do you have that feel familiar or recurring? Have you ever had a dream that felt like a vision from a past life?

_____

_____

_____

_____

_____

_____

_____

_____

_____

_____

What patterns or themes seem to be on repeat in your life, such as relationships, career choices, or personal challenges?

_____

_____

_____

_____

_____

_____

_____

_____

_____

_____

_____

SWEET ALCHEMY

INNER ALCHEMY · TRANSMUTATION

PURIFICATION · INNER LIGHT · CYCLES OF GROWTH

I am ready to transmute the challenges.

I am brilliant, resilient, and perfectly imperfect.

✧ DREAM REFLECTIONS ✧

What do you feel is shifting in your life?

_____
_____
_____
_____
_____
_____
_____
_____
_____
_____

What do you feel is now beginning or being rewoven?

_____
_____
_____
_____
_____
_____
_____
_____
_____
_____

SWEET SURRENDER

LET IT GO · RELEASING EARTHLY ATTACHMENTS

ACTIVATING GRACE · CLEAR THE AIR

I am ready to change things.

I deserve to be fulfilled, happy, and free.

What would I like to surrender or release?

_____
_____
_____
_____
_____
_____
_____
_____
_____
_____

Are there any unhealthy attachments, relationships, or pressures that I am finally ready to vibrate out of my life?

_____
_____
_____
_____
_____
_____
_____
_____
_____

TUNE YOUR FREQUENCY

ENERGY CLEARING · BOUNDARIES

MAGNETISM · CUTTING CORDS · KARMIC PATTERNS

I am ready to amplify my embodiment.

I am in control of the energies I share.

✧ DREAM REFLECTIONS ✧

How am I matching and sharing my own power?

_____

_____

_____

_____

_____

_____

_____

_____

_____

What are my own energetic expectations with my life, my relationships, and my focus?

_____

_____

_____

_____

_____

_____

_____

_____

_____

VISITATION

LOVED ONES · BENEVOLENT GUIDES

REVELATIONS · GUARDIANS

I am blessed with my soul family.

I am open to the beloved signs.

✧ DREAM REFLECTIONS ✧

How can I give thanks and connect with the blessings in my life?

_____

_____

_____

_____

_____

_____

_____

_____

_____

_____

Is there anyone I dream of or ever sense around me?

_____

_____

_____

_____

_____

_____

_____

_____

_____

_____

YOU ARE A GIFT

EMBRACE YOUR UNIQUENESS • INNER GUIDANCE

ADEPT • VISIONARY • STEP INTO YOUR LIGHT

I am always guided by my own strength.

I love the creative way I move through life.

✧ DREAM REFLECTIONS ✧

How am I always being guided back home to myself?

_____

_____

_____

_____

_____

_____

_____

_____

_____

_____

How can I embrace my sensuality, creative nature, and expressive self more?

_____

_____

_____

_____

_____

_____

_____

_____

_____

_____

_____

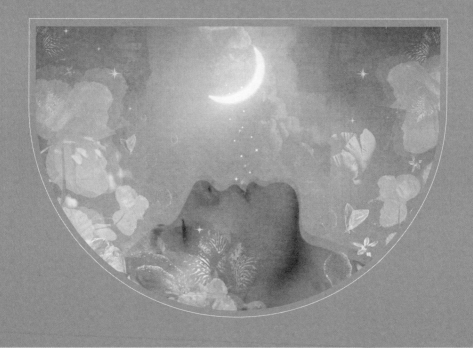

FREE JOURNALING

DATE:

CARD NAME:

DESCRIPTION:

DATE:

CARD NAME:

DESCRIPTION:

DATE:

CARD NAME:

DESCRIPTION:

DATE:

CARD NAME:

DESCRIPTION:

DATE:

CARD NAME:

DESCRIPTION:

DATE:

CARD NAME:

DESCRIPTION:

DATE:

CARD NAME:

DESCRIPTION:

DATE:

CARD NAME:

DESCRIPTION:

CARD NAME:

DESCRIPTION:

DATE:

CARD NAME:

DESCRIPTION:

124

CARD NAME:

DESCRIPTION:

DATE:

CARD NAME:

DESCRIPTION:

DATE:

CARD NAME:

DESCRIPTION:

DATE:

CARD NAME:

DESCRIPTION:

134

DATE:

CARD NAME:

DESCRIPTION:

DATE:

CARD NAME:

DESCRIPTION:

DATE:

CARD NAME:

DESCRIPTION:

DATE:

CARD NAME:

DESCRIPTION:

DATE:

CARD NAME:

DESCRIPTION:

DATE:

CARD NAME:

DESCRIPTION:

DATE:

CARD NAME:

DESCRIPTION:

DATE:

CARD NAME:

DESCRIPTION:

DATE:

CARD NAME:

DESCRIPTION:

DATE:

CARD NAME:

DESCRIPTION:

DATE:

CARD NAME:

DESCRIPTION:

DATE:

CARD NAME:

DESCRIPTION:

DATE:

CARD NAME:

DESCRIPTION:

DATE:

CARD NAME:

DESCRIPTION:

CARD NAME:

DESCRIPTION:

DATE:

CARD NAME:

DESCRIPTION:

DATE:

CARD NAME:

DESCRIPTION: